When the Snowbird Cries

An Intimate Portrait

II

When the Snowbird Cries
An Intimate Portrait

Darnell Dilworth
2017

Copyright © 2017 by Darnell Dilworth

All rights reserved. This book or any portion thereof may not be reproduced or used in any manner whatsoever without the express written permission of the author.

First Printing: 2017

ISBN: 978-1-387-42064-3

Publisher: Darnell Dilworth

Ordering Information:

U.S. trade bookstores and wholesalers: Please contact:

Author: Darnell Dilworth

Business #: (586) 996-8324

Fax#: (248-386-4314

Email address: darnie1219@att.net

Design and layout of this book were done by the Author

Contents

Acknowledgements vii
Preface xi
Introduction 1
Chapter 1: My Roots 3
Chpater 2: The Early Years 15
Chapter 3: My Wedding 27
Chapter 4: Turmoil in my Marriage 39
Chapter 5: Starting Over 49
Chapter 6: Calm Before the Storm 53
Chapter 7: A New Man in my Life 61
Chapter 8: Family Gatherings 67
Chapter 9: The Eighties 75
Chapter 10: Growing Pains 83
Chapter 11: A Geat Lady is Gone 93
Chapter 12: A New Marriage and Farwell 99

Acknowledgements

Thank you, to my loving husband and life partner, without your support and patience I would have never achieved my dream. I love you with all my heart.

I promised myself that I would finish the task my sister Mona Lisa started before her passing when researching our family ancestry. She spent long hours on that project. She wanted to turn her research into a family ancestry book for our whole family. I decided to create a smaller version of her vision with our immediate family starting with our mother and father. I finish it two years ago. The inspiration for this book came from my sister Mona Lisa. I will never forget you and I will always love you.

This is my story.

Preface

In memory of my mother

For all those times you stood by me, for all the truth that you made me see, for all the joy you brought to my life, for all the wrong that you made right, for every dream you made come true, for all the love I found in you, I'll be forever thankful.

You're the one who held me up, never let me fall, You're the one who saw me through it all, you were my strength when I was weak, you were my voice when I couldn't speak, you were my eyes when I couldn't see, you saw the best there was in me, lifted me up when I couldn't reach, you gave me faith because you believed.

I'm everything I am
because you loved me

~ Celine Dion ~

Darnell Dilworth

Introduction

My life has been filled with sorrow, pain, achievements and celebrations. Throughout this book I will chronicle various events that left an emotional impact on my family, my relationships and my life.

This book explores my early childhood and my relationship with a neglectful father, a father who lived in the household but was not there emotionally. I came from a two-parent home, but rarely had the warmth of a loving father as a child. I'm sure that shaped my own relationships with men.

The decisions I made in my life wrote a script I could not imagine for myself or my child.

My remaining siblings, my sister Nkenge Tuck (formerly known as Denise Darcell), brothers Adolph Walker and Glenn Walker. This book is not meant to hurt or embarrass anyone. I only refer to you when it is pertinent to telling my story. I love you all.

My life is now truly an open book.

When the Snowbird Cries

Chapter 1: My Roots

To tell my story I must go back to my roots, where I came from. My family history starts with my grandfather Willis Walker Sr. who was born January 1879 in Stonewall, Mississippi to Steve Walker and Amelia Webb. Willis met and married my grandmother Nora Slaughter in 1910 in Hickory, Mississippi, he was 31 years old and she was 15 years old. My grandfather Willis died at age 48 in 1927.

Nora was the daughter of Adolphus Slaughter and Fannie Dozier. Nora was born October 26, 1895 in Sumter, Alabama and she died at age 44 in 1939. To this union eleven children were born.

My grandmother had two other children by two different men, my aunt Beatrice's father was never known to me and my uncle Arthur's father was A. B. Monk. My aunt Beatrice died 1989 at age 54 and my uncle Arthur died 2014 at age 84

My father was the sixth child born from the union between my grandfather Willis and grandmother Nora. My grandfather had eight other children from other relationships.

I was told my father joined the military at the age of 19.

My mother was born in Choctaw, Alabama and was an only child. My mother lived in Alabama with her grandmother until she was about 14 years.

When the Snowbird Cries

She left Alabama to come to Detroit, Michigan to live with her mother my grandmother (Lula O'Gara).

My parents met in Detroit, Michigan and were married October 1942. My mother being an only child had a lonely childhood and wanted children of her own very badly.

It would be six years before my mother would give birth to her first child. My mom lost her first pregnancy after slipping on ice on a winter's day, I was told it was a boy. She recovered and became pregnant with my sister Johnnie Carol. My Mom would give birth to five more children.

My father   My Mom

I imagine it must have been a cold winter's day when I was born into the world December 1950, a Snowbird. My mother would always ask me which would you prefer, a birthday present or Christmas present.

Darnell Dilworth

In my eyes I always felt I deserved both. According to historical data I was born on a Tuesday and the temperature was in the twenties. My Zodiac chart says my birthday numbers 12, 1950 reveal that my Life Path number is 1. It is initiative, potential and singularity. I am a born leader. I insist on my right to make up my own mind; I demand freedom of thought and action. That describes me very well.

I was the second child born to my mother Helen and father Johnnie Adolphus Walker. My sister Johnnie Carol was born eighteen months earlier. There was some confusion about my name, my father wanted to name me Lee Homa Walker, my mother had other plans she wanted to name me Linda Darnell Walker after the 1940's movie actress Linda Darnell. My grandmother won the battle, I was eventually named Lula Darnell Walker although Lee Homa Walker stayed on the birth certificate until March 1969 the year of my 19th birthday.

I was born in Detroit, Michigan at Wayne Diagnostic Hospital, my mother was 27 years old and my dad was 31 years old.

I don't remember much about my childhood except when I was around two years old my mother left me alone with my sister Mona Lisa who was an infant at the time. My sister Johnnie Carol had started Kindergarten in Detroit and my mother left to go pick her up from school. My sister Mona was left on the bed surrounded by pillows and for some reason I was looking for scissors. I thought I could find them in my father's upright dresser.

When the Snowbird Cries

I pulled out a bottom drawer to stand in and then pulled open the top drawer which made the whole dresser tip over on me. The dresser was near the bed and I was pinned underneath the dresser on the bed, my sister Mona was tossed off the bed and landed between the wall and the bed. When my mother came back home all she heard was crying. I was told I got a well-deserved spanking for that stunt.

I was around three and half years old when my parents bought their first home, and moved the family to Royal Oak Township. The house was built in 1947 and we moved there in 1953 or 1954. There were four children at that time, Johnnie Carol, Lula Darnell (Me), Mona Lisa and Denise Darcell. My brother Adolph Valantio was born 1956. Two years later Glenn Zola was born 1958.

The house we lived in was a small three-bedroom bungalow, as far as I can remember four girls were in one bedroom and the two boys were in the other bedroom across the hall upstairs. My parents occupied the third bedroom downstairs. We had a fun childhood, we grew up in a neighborhood with lots of children. We played in the park down the street every day. The neighborhood was full of at home moms and working dads. Our neighborhood was truly a village.

There wasn't too much we could get away with without a neighbor calling our parents and reporting on us. My sisters and I were labeled Tom Boys because we were rough and tough and did not take a lot of mess from anyone.

My mother raised us to respect our elders, she taught us to address adults as Mr. and Mrs., we replied to them with "Yes Mam" and "Yes Sir".

We were taught not to start fights but we never ran from one. I recall being in the fourth grade and a girl in my class was pulling my hair, pushing me and just taunting me. I did not react because I remember my mother saying if we were caught fighting we would get a spanking. One day sitting at the dinner table one of my siblings started talking about this girl picking on me at school, my mother asked about it and I told her that this girl just did not like me and was pulling on my hair. I had very long hair and my mother braided it in two or three braids with bangs. I told my mother I try to ignore her, but she just would not leave me alone. My mother said; I told you kids not to start fights but I do expect you to defend yourselves. Well that's all I needed, I was given the green light, the next day true to form she came at me again and this time I was ready for her. I let her have it and from that day on she never bothered me again.

When the Snowbird Cries

That taught me to always stand up for myself and NEVER show weakness.

"Knowing when to walk away is WISDOM, being able to is COURAGE, walking away with your head held high is DIGNITY".

The elementary school we attended was Grant Elementary which was built in 1926, it was renovated in 1952 it eventually closed in 1980. It was located on Garden Lane in Ferndale, Michigan. Today the school is used as the Administrative offices for the Township Supervisor and Board of Trustees.

I began going to Grant Elementary the fall of 1956, that year I would turn six years old in December. I should have started school in 1955 but there was a rule that a child would have to turn five years old by December 1st to start Kindergarten in September, my birth date fell after the 1st so my mother had to wait another year for me to start Kindergarten.

My memory of my first day of school is fuzzy but I recall lots of kids crying as their mothers left them. I think I was in shock but to scare to cry.

I remember a teacher by the name of Mr. Crittenden. He used a paddle on kids who misbehaved. I never got in trouble because I would get it again from my parents when I got home. One-day Mr. Crittenden came over to me and ask me where were my glasses. I wore glasses but did not like to wear them. I told him they were in my pocket, he said come to his desk, he made me pull my skirt tight and he hit me two times with the paddle. He told me to put my glasses on and keep them on. I always wore my glasses in his class after that.

I discovered some historical information about my elementary school online from "The Crow's Nest" newsletter written by Chris Hammer in 2013.

Grant Elementary School

THE DESEGREGATION OF FERNDALE SCHOOLS

Like many cities in the region and the country, Ferndale has not been immune to racial tensions and controversies over the years. In fact, Ferndale was the first northern school district ever to be found in violation of civil rights laws by the United States Department of Health, Education, and Welfare. The federal government claimed in the late

1960s that the Ferndale School District's Grant Elementary School, built in Royal Oak Township in 1926, was built as an exclusively African-American school.

Over the next decade, litigation ensued, culminating in a federal court's order in 1980 to integrate Grant with two other schools in the district. From its earliest days, the Ferndale School District included the African-American part of Royal Oak Township near Eight Mile and Wyoming. Several factors reinforced the racial divide between the growing communities of Ferndale and Royal Oak Township during the 1920s, 1930s, and 1940s.

The Federal Housing Administration policies limited mortgage funds available to racially integrated neighborhoods. In addition, most of the residential properties in Ferndale had restrictive covenants forbidding their owners from selling their property to African-American citizens. Oakland County courts routinely enforced those covenants until the United States Supreme Court ruled, in the 1948 decision of Shelley v. Kraemer, that their enforcement was unconstitutional. Homes in Royal Oak Township were not similarly restricted but, as a result, many white families looked elsewhere when deciding where to live.

As the village, and later city, of Ferndale grew during the 1920s, the School District built seven new elementary schools: Harding (1920), Roosevelt (1920), Washington (1923), Wilson (1923), Coolidge (1925), Jefferson (1925), and Grant (1926). In 1925, the Ferndale

School District approved a neighborhood schools plan for all the children in the District. Each child would attend an elementary school with in one half mile from home.

As part of the neighborhood schools plan, Jefferson opened in 1925 as an integrated school that served both Royal Oak Township and the southwest part of Ferndale. Jefferson's attendance for the 1925-26 school year was 297, including 101 African-American children (34%). However, citing turmoil at Jefferson, the School Board authorized Grant as an annex to Jefferson. Grant would not have its own principal. Instead, Jefferson's principal would continue to oversee Grant.

The Board selected boundaries for Grant that included only African-American neighborhoods (including the Forest Grove and Detroyal subdivisions).

Shortly after it opened, Superintendent Edgar Down publicly stated that Grant was the District's "colored" school and that it was unique in that regard. In fact, it was the only school in the District to employ African-American teachers until 1949, and it did not employ any white teachers or full-time staff until 1952. Additionally, Grant was overcrowded for many years, even while other elementary schools (including Jefferson) had excess capacity.

While the District often transferred students from overcrowded

When the Snowbird Cries

schools to balance the size of its classes, the District did not move Grant students to nearby schools for fear of the "turmoil" that would result, according to Superintendent Down. Of course, the "separate but equal" doctrine then in force allowed school districts to keep separate facilities for white students and for African-American students. Nevertheless, even after Brown v. Board of Education (1954) ruled that separate schools were inherently unequal, the District maintained neighborhood boundary lines that resulted in the continued segregation of Grant.

Lincoln Jr. High was built in April 1919 and the first section of the school was completed by 1920. Over several years other sections would be added to complete the complex.

Lincoln Jr. High School in Ferndale, Michigan

Darnell Dilworth

By 1963 students from Grant school were being sent to Lincoln Jr. High school located at Nine Mile and Livernois.

I began the seventh grade there. In November of 1963 while in my math class an announcement came over the P. A. system. The voice said President John F. Kennedy had been assassinated. The classroom got quiet and my teacher began to cry. I was twelve years old at that time, I would celebrate my thirteenth birthday the following month.

When I got home from school that day my parents were watching the news, the atmosphere was as though a member of our family had died. I could not understand why my parents felt so bad about the death of this man. I later realized that my mother felt President John F. Kennedy believed in equals rights for all people including African Americans.

When the Snowbird Cries

Chapter 2: The Early Years

Growing up in the sixties was a fun time for me, we had one television in our home and we loved watching American Bandstand, Father Knows Best, Donna Reed, Ed Sullivan etc. My mother usually sat down and watched the programs with us. We spent most of our time with my mother. My father spent a lot of time away from home. We were all afraid of my father, he hardly ever had a nice word for us. There were times when watching a TV show, we would hear my father's car pull into the driveway, everyone would get up and run upstairs. My mother spent all her time attending to us and the household. She was a great mother, always there for us. She only had a third-grade education, my father finished the eighth grade.

I remember when my mother started night school to learn how to read and write. We would help her with her lessons. She eventually finished her classes and she began to read Perry Mason novels. I remember one time she had started one of her novels and she was telling us about it and how she could not wait to find out who the killer was, well one of us I can't remember who flipped through the book and found out who the killer was and told my mother, she was so disappointed. I think she started hiding her books after that. I grew up seeing and hearing my father abuse my mother. I promised myself I would never let that happen to me.

When the Snowbird Cries

Our house was very small, so you can imagine how us kids got on each other's nerves. I would have fights with my sisters and brothers as most kids did but I don't think anyone held a grudge. My mother did not allow fighting and when caught we got a spanking.

My mother also did not excuse lying. If one of us did something but did not tell the truth about it my mother would spank us all. I never thought that was fair.

When we became adults sitting around talking about the good old days, my brothers and sisters would say how they would take spankings for me because they hated to see me cry. Somehow, I don't remember it that way.

It was always loud in our household, I never liked a lot of noise. When I needed to be by myself I would go to a closet and hide in the back of it for peace and quiet. When I was gone too long my mother would ask everyone if they knew where I was, the answer would be "No mom I have not seen her". Then my mother would say, "check the closets" and there I would be fast asleep.

I was a quiet child and out of all my sisters and brothers I always felt different. I would sit on our front porch at night in the summer and think about life and why God made me. I would think about what happens to people when they die. I thought about it after my grandmother died but I really started to think about it after my aunt Drucilla died.

She was my father's sister who came to live with us for a very short time. I remember my mother saying she was sick, but I never knew what was wrong with her. My aunts and uncles would always say how much I looked like my aunt Drucilla.

My aunt Drucilla eventually moved out and went to California where she died at age 40, that year I would celebrate my 14th birthday in December. As a child you think only old people die but later as I got older I would come to know that was not true.

My Aunt Drucilla   Darnell (at age 36)

My mother always made the holidays very special for us, my Dad would bring home the tree and we would try and help my mother decorate it, if my father helped I don't remember.

I remember one Christmas Eve as a child my mother let us watch our favorite programs on television then we had to take our baths and get

When the Snowbird Cries

ready for bed, so Santa Claus could come. She said he would only come once we were asleep. I think I was about ten or eleven years old.

We had taken our baths and was upstairs in our beds but still talking about what we wanted Santa Claus to bring us. Suddenly, the doorbell rang. We heard my mother shout out "go away Santa my children are not asleep yet, you will have to come back if you can" we shouted down to my mother "we going to sleep right now momma" and everyone was quiet. Christmas morning finally came, and we were always up before my parents.

We would run downstairs and see all the presents under the tree. I would not realize until I was an adult how great a sacrifice it was for my parents to buy all the toys and clothes for the six of us. My mother wasn't working, and my father was the sole provider in our family at that time. I realized then that's how my father loved us, by sacrifice and hard work to support our household.

I would like to believe the anger my father showed us was because he had sacrificed his dreams of being an Artist. I was told my dad was in Art School before any us were born. I was told when my mother found out that part of his studies was drawing live nude women, she was not happy. I don't know if that was the reason he quit. I think he had ambitions that were never realized for whatever reason. I know the needs of the family took precedence.

Darnell Dilworth

My dad worked as a security guard for Big Boys, and then Arlans department store. Growing up my siblings and I thought my dad was a policeman because of the uniform he wore. There were others who thought the same. I remember when someone shot a gun through our living room window almost hitting me and my little brother Glenn.

I was in a rocking chair near the window and my little brother was walking back and forth across the floor handing my mother sections of newspapers. My mother was sitting on the couch clipping coupons. I was around eight years old and my brother was two years old.

Later my mother found out that some white boys from the Ferndale side of town had been stopped by the Royal Oak Township police force for speeding down Northend street the road right by our house.

It was thought they saw my father leaving for work in his security guard uniform and mistaken him for a policeman working in Royal Oak Township. My dad worked in Detroit.

When the Snowbird Cries

Dad in the Military   Security Guard Uniform

As an adolescent I had a few puppy love boyfriends. The first boy I ever thought of as a boyfriend was a neighborhood boy by the name of Dennis Cochran. It was only a summer fling, I was twelve. The next boy I thought I was in love with was Lawrence Davis who came to visit his aunt and uncle across the street from our house, that did not last long either. In middle school (Lincoln Jr High) there was Tyrone Lewis, he played on the basketball team and he lasted a little longer. He would become a friend of the family.

My first year of high school was the fall of 1966, I was a freshman at Ferndale High located in Ferndale, Michigan.

My freshman year was a little scary to me, although my Junior high school classmates followed me to Ferndale, it was still a mostly all white high school. It took a while, but I eventually began to make friends with some of the white students. Although it was 1966 I felt the black students were being tolerated but not really excepted. I remember two of my girlfriends and I auditioning for the Eagle Eye review (A Talent Show). This Talent Show was held every year and black students always auditioned for it, but were never excepted. We eventually had our own Talent Show at the old elementary school (Grant).

As I became acclimated into my new high school I became interested in a boy who was the neighborhood newspaper boy. After a week or two it was over.

I was not a girl who like boys that tried to manage me, I did not like boys who thought they could tell me what to do. I would carry those feelings well into my adulthood.

During the summer of 1967 a boy caught my eye, his name was John Wesley Ross Jr. He had already graduated from Ferndale High School. He was a member of a neighborhood singing group called the "Irresistibles", and he was three years older than I was. I really loved the Temptations at that time and his group sang a lot of the Temptation's songs. The group sang at all the neighborhood Talent Shows and I tried to be at all of them.

I later discovered that John was the cousin of two of best friends (Vicki Rice and Rene Tillis). I would see him walking in the neighborhood and one day I was at Rene's house and he was there. We struck up a conversation and for a while I would meet him at Rene's house until my mother found out.

Once that happened I thought it was over, but my mother surprised me, she said I was old enough to date but he would have to come to our house to see me. During that time, we followed the Muslim faith and I could only have male friends over when my parents were home.

I remember one-day John wanted to take me to the Dairy Queen in our neighborhood but the only way I could go was to take my brother Adolph with me.

Sometime later I remember something had happened concerning my relationship with John that my mother did not like. She and I had an argument about it. She told me I could not see him anymore.

I was crying my eyes out in a back room in our house while ironing some clothes. I heard my Dad coming down the hall from our living room. You could always hear my Dad walking because he dragged his right leg due to a stroke. He came into the room and put his arms around me and gave me a big hug. My father had never done that before. He said, "It's okay daddy understands how you feel". That was the first time my dad had shown me true affection. My father's affection meant a lot to me, I have never forgotten that day.

Darnell Dilworth

I dated John all through high school. He took me to both my Junior and Senior Proms. We dated five years before he asked me to marry him.

Ferndale High June 1969

John and I at my Junior and Senior Prom

When the Snowbird Cries

After graduating I followed my older sister Johnnie Carol to Oakland Community College in Farmington Hills. I really enjoy my college days there, we met black students who were involved in the Black movement going on at the time. Shortly after I started college a neighbor told my mother that Michigan Bell Telephone Company was hiring. She knew my mother had two daughters that recently graduated, and it could be an opportunity for us to land a job. I don't really remember why my sister Carol did not put in an application, but I did. I did not think I would get called but three weeks after putting in the application I got a call to come down for an interview.

I remember being very excited and nervous at the same time. The day of my interview I remember the weather being very windy. I was told the day of my interview that I had the job. I was sent over to another building for a physical (The Leland House on Bagley).

Later, that day after returning home my mother told me she heard on the news that a construction worker fell to his death from the roof of the same building I had just left.

I was hired February 1971 as a Junior File Clerk working in Central Records in the Engineering Department in Southfield, Michigan. My first assignment was delivering mail to all the Division and District level managers. I would load a cart and drop off the mail at their Secretary's desk.

There were three floors in my building, it was a lot of walking, but I still dressed the part. I wore suits, dresses and high heels which was the business attire at that time. It would be years later before women could wear pants suits.

One day while on my route I saw a very handsome Engineer Trainee who caught my eye. Although I had just got engage two months before being hired, I still reserved the right to recognize very handsome men when I saw them. I asked around and found out his name was Raymond. I did not realize this man would play a very important role in my life years later.

My first friend at the company was a woman named Vie Harris, she was much older than me.

I was just two months into my 20th birthday. I think Vie was about thirty-six. She really looked after me and showed the ropes about my job and the right and wrong people to be involved with.

I thought she was very pretty, she stood about five feet – two and was very light skinned with freckles and red hair. I remember she was confronted by a woman who worked down the hall from us. She thought Vie was messing around with her boyfriend. In those days Michigan Bell was like Peyton Place, everybody was in someone else's business. When Vie and I went out for lunch one day I asked her if she would fight the lady who confronted her, she told me "I am too little to be fighting someone" then she open her purse and show me a small gun. I knew then she was no one to mess with.

I later met a young woman who would become a close friend, she was three years younger than me. Her name was Phinell Boykin. We were labeled the bobbsey twins, Darnell and Phinell. We became very close and would hang out together at work and after work. I don't see much of her today, but she remains a very dear friend.

Chapter 3: My Wedding

On August 1971 I married John Wesley Ross Jr. I was the only daughter my father would walk down the aisle. I did not have the traditional wedding in a church because we never belonged to one. My mother started going to my grandmother's church when I was very little. When we moved to the suburbs we stopped going.

My mother started following the Muslim faith in the early sixties. I was around twelve or thirteen at the time. As I got older and began dating John, I discovered I was expected to marry a Muslim man, I left the Mosque at age 18.

I had my wedding at home, my mother and father could not afford to finance a big wedding. My mother was not that happy about the fact I was marrying John, but she did everything she could to help make my wedding day beautiful.

My dear sister Johnnie Carol was my Maid of Honor and three childhood girlfriends were my Brides Maids (Vicki Rice, Rene Tillis and Marva Lewis). I made my wedding dress and Carol made her Maid of Honor's dress.

My friend Vicki Rice would lose her battle from complications of Sarcoidosis in 2008.

When the Snowbird Cries

John Cleary was the Best Man. I remember worrying about the weather that day, rain was in the forecast. The rain held off.

Darnell Dilworth

My sister Johnnie Carol and me

When the Snowbird Cries

I was finally Mrs. Lula Darnell Ross. Being raised with a strict upbringing, I was taught to abstain from sex until marriage. I followed my mother's rules, I was a virgin when I married John. Our honeymoon was put on hold because of finances.

One month after my Wedding my mother called me on the phone and said my father had been diagnosed with lung cancer. He was given only seven months to live. I was shocked, I never thought I would lose my father so soon. In mid-September of 1971 he was admitted to Henry Ford Hospital on Grand Blvd. in Detroit, Michigan. He would never leave.

One morning in November 1971, I woke to realize it was my sister Denise's birthday. I got up, got dress and told my husband I was going to the Mall to buy my sister a birthday present. I don't remember what I finally purchased but I was in J L Hudson's standing at the gift wrap counter when I started to feel funny. I was starting to see spots before my eyes and felt very warm.

I finally reached the counter when the lady asked me which wrap I wanted, that's all I remember. The next thing I knew I was opening my eyes with a lot of people looking down on me. I had fainted, and I was on the floor with a woman asking me "are you okay dear". I was helped up and put into a wheel chair, I was taken to the front door, so I could get some air. A lady kept asking me "are you pregnant dear", I told her I don't know.

Another lady came over and told me who should they call to come pick me up, I told her my husband. I gave her my phone number. A little later she came back and said, "I called your husband and he kept saying "she has the car, she has the car". He finally picked me up after contacting his best friend John Cleary.

I went to my doctor and was told I was eight weeks pregnant. When I told my mother and father they were very happy. I think my father was happier because I don't think he thought he would live long enough to see his first grandchild.

Fast forward nine months later exactly three months before my son was born my Dad finally passed away from lung cancer in February 1972. My Dad and I were not very close, but I loved him just the same. My mother was devastated.

Three months later May 1972 after twenty-three hours of labor I gave birth to a baby boy, we named him SeQuan Edward Ross. He was given the middle name Edward from my husband's best friend John Edward Cleary.

I enjoyed being a mother, I was very protective of my son. I tried to do everything the doctor told me to do. During that time in the 70's, a new mother was expected to keep her newborn away from being exposed to the public until the baby had their first set of shots. So, the only people allowed to come and visit during the six-week period was my mother and my mother-in law.

When the Snowbird Cries

My mother was a proud grandma, my son was her first grandchild. She was the only person trusted with my baby.

I only took three months for maternity leave because we were saving for a house. I had a close relationship with my Supervisor (Judy Hartline) and she periodically called me to find out if I was ready to come back to work. She would inform me about upcoming job openings.

John and I lived in an apartment on Greenfield in Detroit, Michigan north of Fenkell. John decorated our apartment in an Egyptian motif. There were some wild colors going on, but it was fine at the time.

When I decided to go back to work I needed a babysitter, since my younger sister was not working my mother suggested I let her take care of my son. It did not work out, so my mother spoke to a neighbor that lived on the next street behind my mother's house. We grew up calling her and her husband Auntie Marie and Uncle Dean. She became my babysitter and my son could not have been in better hands other than my Mother.

Shortly after returning to work I was promoted to General Office Clerk in the Customer Service Department. My new Supervisor was a very nice older man (Harry Sherwin).

He was nice to me and respectful. I would not be so fortunate later in my career. Two years after my son was born John and I could afford the honeymoon we never had. We also bought a three-bedroom house in Detroit, Michigan

We decided to take a trip to Hawaii, I always wanted to go and so did my mother. John and I decided to take my mother and my son. It was the summer of 1974 when we took off for Hawaii. We toured two islands (Hawaii and Oahu). We went on day tours and during the evening my Mom watched our son while we soaked up the nightlife.

We enjoyed the trip and now we were home moving into our new house. We moved the fall of 1974, I loved decorating my son's room. John and I found decals of large jungle animals at Sears to put on his walls. Our house became the home I always dreamed of and for a time I was very happy.

My baby and me   My mother with my son

When the Snowbird Cries

By this time, my marriage and my job were going well. Michigan Bell initiated a new hire campaign, they were asking employees to submit names of people looking for employment. I submitted my youngest sister's name (Denise Darcel). She recently graduated from high school and was still unemployed. I submitted her name and she was called for an interview. She was hired as a Telephone Operator, I was so excited for her. After a week or so I called my mother to find out how she was enjoying her new job. My mother told me she

34

worked for two or three days and quit. I was disappointed, I thought it was a great opportunity for her.

I'm a new Mom, Wife and Working girl, things were great. In those days discrimination in the work place was prevalent. I remember there was an opening for District Secretary and the qualifications for this position was being able to take Shorthand. I did not qualify but I knew black women who had the skill. When it came down to filling the job, the District level selected a white female from the Steno pool (a department that processed large typing jobs).

I was told she did not know Shorthand and could hardly type. What she did have was long blonde hair, blue eyes and big boobs. She was notorious for going out on the lawn at lunch time, putting down a blanket and sun tanning herself.

Her promotion caused so much friction among the black employees the EEOC (Equal Employment Opportunity Commission) was called in. After a year or so she eventual got married and left the company. I kept my head up and performed my job as best as I could.

Sometime later my younger sister Mona Lisa met someone by the name of Lumumba Gordan. One-day she announced that she was engaged, I was very happy for her. I was puzzled by the announcement because everyone knew how much she cared for a guy by the name of Dexter Scott. We were all surprised when she showed up with her

When the Snowbird Cries

new man. She decided on an Afro Wedding and I was one of her bride's maids. It was a lovely wedding and she seemed very happy.

Darnell Dilworth

When the Snowbird Cries

Darnell Dilworth

Chapter 4: Turmoil in my Marriage

Four years into my marriage I started to feel like something was missing. My husband was a great provider, but our relationship did not satisfy me. I would hear other women talk about their sex lives and it was nothing like what I had at home. I thought I had a normal marriage, but I had nothing to compare my sexual relationship with because he was my first. I started to feel like my husband was losing interest in me. We were only in our twenties and I could not understand what was wrong. The men at work were constantly chasing after me but I shut them down because I was devoted to my marriage and family. I remember going in for a check-up one day with my GYN Dr. Robinson, he was like a father to me. I don't know how the conversation started but I asked him about why I might be feeling unsatisfied in my sex life. My doctor asked how often did we have sexual relations, I told him "Maybe once every two or three months". My doctor said couples in their sixties have sex more than that. He offered some advice on how to spice things up and that I should go home and try it.

One day I called my mother and asked her if she would keep my son overnight. I went out and I bought a sexy nightie, came home showered and was waiting for my husband to come home from work. When he got there, I had soft music playing with wine and glasses by the bed.

When the Snowbird Cries

He immediately got in the shower and then came into the bedroom. We started to make love, but nothing was happening. He told me, "when I'm expected to perform, I can't".

I brushed it off and said "that's okay, you're just tired. I felt there was something about me that was not attractive to him. Years later I would find out it was not me. I cried myself to sleep that night.

As time went on I made my marriage and my son my life. My husband was a good provider who was a hard worker and helped me around the house. On Saturday mornings he would help me clean the house and do laundry. He would even cook dinner on occasion. We were compatible in every regard except sexually.

I dedicated myself to be a good mother, I had a good role model. I wanted the best for my son, when he was three and a half I put my son in a Head Start program. I found an all-day program on Wyoming in Detroit.

One day I came to pick him up and when I came through the door I smelled smoke and when I walked in further I saw the ceilings ripped out, wires hanging all over the place, water flooding the floors. There had been a fire, and no one was in the building. I ran out the door wondering where was my baby. A lady was walking towards me carrying her child, she told me "If you are looking for your child, they took them to the building down the street".

Darnell Dilworth

I ran to the building she had left and a young woman who was an assistant met me at the door. She said, "Your child is fine we had an electrical fire. We got them all out, we were lucky they were not taking their naps, or it might have been worst waking them and getting them all out". A teacher heard the young lady telling me this and came over and rushed her away. I was fuming at this point. I asked the teacher why didn't anyone call me to let me know something had happened, she said there was no time. My son never went back to that facility. I found another Day Care facility on Greenfield, north of Seven Mile called the Michigan Institute. He was there until he started kindergarten.

By this time my marriage was on the rocks and I did not know how to fix it. I could tell my husband had no sexual desire for me. I worked from 8:30am to 5:00pm, and after work I picked up my son from Day Care, went home and got started on dinner. The three of us would always have dinner together, after dinner I would do dishes, bathe my son and get him ready for bed. I was no longer a happy wife.

It's early 1975, my husband and I are starting to stray further and further apart. I was slowly moving up at work little promotions were coming my way and that's when I really started to regret not completing college. In those days if you did not have a degree, you needed a sponsor. I was now an Administrative Office Assistant working in the Outside Plant Department.

When the Snowbird Cries

One day a young man followed me down the hall and asked me for my name, I told him. He was very flirtatious, and I liked it. He had beautiful brown eyes, about 6' 2" tall and slim. I was attracted to him right away. He had a lot of women going crazy over him, he eventually got tagged with the nickname "Mr. Charisma", it suited him very well. He would later nickname me "Legs". I was 5' 4" tall weighing 125 lbs. I wore my dresses and skirts above my knee. It was still respectable and business like. The man I am referring to is now married and out of respect for his wife I will not mention his real name in this book, I will call him Brad.

Brad and I would see each other at lunch in the cafeteria, he would be sitting with a group of friends and sometimes I would join them. It got to the point I could not wait to get to work in the morning hoping I would see him. The flirting continued but he kept a safe distance because I was married.

I don't know how or who started it but every Friday after work a bunch of us would meet at a place called Jazz Workshop on Schaefer in Detroit. Someone started calling it Choir Rehearsal. I started stopping by before going home. I did not drink alcohol, but I would stop by for a Coke and visit with my co-workers. It was a chance to unwind and enjoy some music.

I would see Brad at the Jazz Workshop, he would ask me to dance and then we would sit and talk. I really had fun being there with him. He was a great dancer, I loved slow dancing with him. He would hold me very close to him, I could feel his heart beating, or it could have been my heart. Every part of my body tingled. Later it was time for me to leave and go home to my son and a husband who had no desire for me. There was no romance in my marriage

My feelings for him were changing and I would hear rumors about my husband being a homosexual. I never believe it but then again it would explain why my marriage was in the shape it was in. I began to wear light makeup, something I never did much of. It made me feel better about myself. I remember one day coming home and John asked me about the makeup. He said to me "take it off, I don't want you wearing makeup" I told him he was not my father and I will wear what I want to wear. I went down to the living room and laid on the couch to read a magazine. John came down to the living room with a soapy face cloth and started washing my face real hard. I jumped up and asked him what the hell was wrong with him. I ran back upstairs to wash the soap out of my eyes. After washing my face, I started to put my makeup back on, the next thing I knew I was seeing stars. He had hit me in the face, I told him "you have just signed your divorce papers". I tried to get my son and leave but he refused to let me take him. I left the house anyway.

I ended up at a friend's house, her name was Connie Reddix. I told her what happened, and she told me, "I understand what you are feeling but if you don't go back he could have you charged with abandonment". I did not want him to have sole custody of my son, so I went home. John slept in my son's room that night and the next morning he took him to Day Care.

I went to my mother house the next day and told her what had happened. I told her about the state of my marriage and about the rumors of him being gay. I told my mother I was trying to live up to my vows; "For better or for worst" but it was really starting to get to me. I expected my mother to be surprised but she wasn't. She told me she always had a feeling about John and that he was not the right one for me. I asked my mother what should I do, she told me "if you want to get a divorce I will help you". My mother contacted the attorney who helped litigate my younger brother's case when he got in some trouble in high school.

I filed for divorce and waited for my husband to be served with the papers. When he was finally served he was asked to move out. I remember the day he started moving his things out, his mother and his brother Dorian came to our house. I didn't know if they were there to help him move or ride shot gun. I know his mother was there to watch me.

When we were official separated I felt free, I felt like a burden had been lifted and I could start my life all over again with my son. By November of 1975 one month before my twenty-fifth birthday I was

Darnell Dilworth

taking Business Administration courses at Detroit College of Business in Dearborn. I was going through a divorce, maintaining a home on my own, taking care of a three-year-old and working. I would take my son to school, be at work by 8:30am, and worked until 5:00pm After work I would pick up my son from school, bring him home, fix dinner, drop him off at my mother's house and make my first class by 7:00pm. My last class was over at 10:00pm. I would leave my son at my mother's house when I was too tired to pick him up. I did this for two years to give myself a better chance for a promotion.

Brad and I were starting to see more of each other, but I had no right to expect he was all mine because by law I was still married. Until I was divorced I knew we could not be considered a couple. We would sometimes meet at my girlfriend's apartment (Connie Reddix), she was dating his brother. In the fall of 1975 the Isley Brothers recorded a song called "For the love of you". Every time that song was played no matter where we were we would dance together. There were times the song would be playing, and we were across the room somewhere, we would find each other and dance to the record.

As time passed we really started to connect, at least in my mind. He invited me to his apartment one day for drinks and conversation. That night we made love for the first time. I finally knew what real love making was all about. By the middle of 1976 I was seeing Brad on a regular basis, but my divorce was not final.

When the Snowbird Cries

Something happened quite unexpectedly, I started feeling like something was different with me. I realized my period was late. I made an appointment with my doctor and he told me I was twelve weeks pregnant. I was happy and devastated at the same time. It couldn't have come at a worst time in my life. How would I explain carrying another man's baby in divorce court? I was afraid I would lose custody of my son and custody would be granted to my husband. I was not going to let that happen.

I made the decision to have an abortion and end the pregnancy. My heart was broken, I cried so hard I thought my eyes would bleed. This Snowbird was devastated.

By November 1976 I had a final court date for my divorce. The judge asked both of us if there was any chance of reconciliation, there wasn't. When I walked out of court that day I was a divorced woman with sole custody of my son. I was twenty-five soon to celebrate my twenty-sixth birthday the following month and I was a single mother on my own.

A year later I was talking to one of my girlfriends who lived in my old neighborhood. She confirmed my suspicions about my ex-husband's sexuality. She told me he is now dating another man. My ex-husband and his partner have been together now 41 years. He found his true soul mate.

Darnell Dilworth

My family photo with my Son

When the Snowbird Cries

I really enjoyed being a mommy

Chapter 5: Starting Over

I was free to date Brad out in the open but for some reason he still wanted to keep us a secret. He claimed it was due to our jobs, not wanting the workplace gossip to start about us. I agreed with him because there was a lot of gossiping going on at that time. Someone was calling the homes of married couples and telling their spouses about what the other was doing.

One day I was at the Jazz Workshop with Brad and my girlfriend Connie was there sitting with another male engineer who I will not name. Her husband walked in with a camera and took a picture of her sitting with this engineer. Then he grabs her and pulled her out of the club. I tried calling her the next day, but I never got an answer back. She took off from work and no one knew how she was doing. I soon received a call from her and I went over to her mother's house where she was staying. When I got there, I could see the bruises on her face, arms and chest. She told me she and her husband had fought. That ended her marriage.

So, I was all for keeping my relationship with Brad secret from the workplace gossip. Sometime later I found out it was not just because of gossip, he was seeing other women.

One day he asked me if I was going to Choir Rehearsal, I told him no I was tired, and I would be going home after work.

When the Snowbird Cries

When I got home and relaxed for a while I decided to go. When I got there another man by the name of Jay Trent stopped me and ask me to dance with him, so I did. By this time Brad had spotted me and came over to where I was dancing. After Jay and I finished dancing Brad took me to another table and we sat down.

He said to me "I thought you weren't coming" I told him I changed my mind. Brad stayed with me for the rest of the night and when I got ready to go home, he said he would follow me back to my house.

I got home and was waiting for him. It took about an hour for him to show up. I later find out that he was with someone else at the club before I got there. She got upset and started to drink very heavily. He was told she was in the lady's room throwing up and he wanted to make sure she got home safely. It would be a year later before I found out about that night and who she was.

By now Brad and I were becoming very close, I remember when Brad's District manager was having a dinner party for all his engineers. Brad's boss lived in Northville and Brad wanted me to go with him. I told him it sounds kind of fancy and I don't have anything nice to wear. Brad told me that was not a problem, he took me to the Mall and I tried on several dresses until Brad said that's the one. He bought the dress and I went to the dinner party, I felt very special that night.

Darnell Dilworth

Life was good, everything was going smoothly, my mother was in good health, and she was enjoying her only grandchild.

In 1977, I did something stupid. I went out and purchased a new car. It was a Canary yellow 280Z sports car. Brad drove one and I decided I wanted one. The cost $7,300.00 brand new, keep in mind this is the price in the 1970's. Later I began to struggle financially.

In my divorce decree John would pay $25.00 a month in child support. I had to repay him his part of the down payment for the house we purchased together. Therefore, there was no child support because I was just returning the money he gave me. He also asked for my wedding ring set, although by law I did not have to return the rings I gave them to him anyway, I wanted to just be done with him. I thought everything was settled between my ex-husband and I could move forward with my life. I should have known that was too good to be true.

When the Snowbird Cries

I thought I wanted to be a Model

Chapter 6: The Calm before the storm

I was working hard and living my life. One day I came home and retrieved the mail. I saw an envelope that looked like it was from an attorney's office, it was. I opened it and my ex-husband was suing me for joint custody. Someone told him if he had joint custody he would not have to pay child support. He wanted to make sure I was not benefitting from the little money he was paying me.

I had to go back to court and fight for custody. The court ordered a home visit of both homes and mediation. In the end we both ended up with joint custody. My son would spend six months with his father and six months with me. We agreed on a school that he would remained in no matter who he was with.

I would like to say this was the end of my court battles over child custody but about a year later I was sent more court papers regarding sole custody. I was not financially able to afford an attorney. I was crying to Brad about it and he said to me "Do you want your Son?" I told him, of course. He said then don't worry about hiring an attorney I will pay for it. I was so relieved that I had someone in my corner.

My son is six years old and I have been separated and divorced now three years. We met with the Mediator and at one point I lost it. I told the Mediator, "How long will I have to put up with this before

When the Snowbird Cries

someone say enough is enough, I have been back and forth in court with my ex-husband ever since I divorced him, I want this to end"

The Mediator made the decision that nothing needed to change and told both of us that unless something major happened where one of us was physically unable to take care of our son this was the end.

"A Birthday Party for my Little Boy"

Darnell Dilworth

After my court date was over I called Brad and told him the hearing was over. The Mediator warned my ex-husband not to bring another action against me unless something drastic happened. I was finally able to live my life without his interference.

I am seeing Brad on a regular basis, my girlfriend Connie is dating his brother. I was at her apartment one day and Brad's brother was there. Later Brad came over, we talked, played cards and danced to music. It started to get late and I thought Brad would be coming back to my house. He told me he had something else he had to do, and he left. Eventually his brother left as well. I was sad that Brad could not come back to my house with me but then Connie told me something that I was not expecting to hear. She said he was going over his ex-girlfriend's house. She was pregnant, and she finally told him he was going to be a father. I was devastated, my heart was broken. I asked Connie, "are you sure" she said yes. I didn't believe it, so I asked her if she knew the girlfriend's address.

She told me, and I left her apartment to go and see if he was with her. I got to her house and his car was in the driveway. I left and drove home crying all the way.

My son was at his father's house, so I was all alone in the house. My heart was broken. My luck with men was not the greatest. I took the next day off from work. My phone was ringing all day, but I did not answer it. Later that evening I called Connie and she told me Brad

When the Snowbird Cries

was trying to get in touch with me. I told her, I did not want to talk to him. Later that night I finally answered the phone and spoke with Brad, he told me he had broken up with his ex-girlfriend but later found out she was pregnant. I asked him what was he going to do, he said he would take care of his obligation with her, but he was not going back to her. I believed him.

We continued seeing each other and our relationship was in a good place for a while, then another shoe dropped.

It is the summer of 1977 and I am working at the American Motors building. A new hire began working in Brad's department she and I became friends. We began having coffee and lunch together at work. I would sometime have a bunch of co-workers over my house after work to hang out, talk, play music and have fun.

I remember one time a bunch of us went up to Ford Lake for a picnic and I was going with Brad. An Engineer who was married and had a small boat was taking the boat up to the lake to teach us how to water ski. The Engineer was Raymond Dilworth Jr. He was the engineer I spotted on my mail routes years ago when I started working at the company. Raymond also had a motorcycle that Brad wanted to try out.

Brad once owned a motorcycle as well and had not been on one for a long time. I wanted to ride up to the lake with him, but he told me to wait for the ride back. He needed to get familiar with the motorcycle. We had lots of fun that day, I tried water skiing but was unsuccessful. I was the only female that tried it. By the end of the day everyone was starting to leave, and I rode back on the motorcycle with Brad, it was exhilarating.

We got back to Raymond's house and dropped off the motorcycle, we left and went back to Brad's house. When we got to the house he said he was not feeling well so I went home. Sometime later I found out he was lying, and the new female hire who pretended to be my friend was coming in the back door while I was walking out the front.

Brad and I were having problems, he told me that I deserved someone better, someone who could offer me more than he could give at the time. He told me he had decided to marry his ex-girlfriend who had just given birth to a son.

He said he still loved me and he was only marrying her, so he could have a relationship with his son. We broke up.

I buried myself into taking care of my son, going to school and work. I would visit my mother on the weekends and by this time, I have a two-year-old Nephew, his name was Neequeem. My mother really loved having her grandchildren around.

I began to shop a lot, it helped me with my depression. I thought buying new clothes and making myself look good would make me feel better about myself. My life started to spiral out of control. I was spending money I did not have, I was using credit cards to buy unnecessary things. I became a financial mess. I had to get a hold of my finances.

On occasion I did not have money for groceries, so I would make scrambled eggs and pancakes for dinner. I thought about what my mother did for us growing up when she had no money. My mother would feed us meals that were thought of as breakfast for dinner all the time and none of us went to bed hungry and neither did my son.

I was at a low point in my life and feeling very depressed. One day, a new Engineer started working in the department next door to me. He came over to introduce himself, "Hi, my name is Nicholas Harris, what's your name". I told him my name and we went to the café for coffee. We hit it off and we became good friends. He had just graduated with an Electrical Engineering Degree from the University of Michigan. He was 6' 5" tall, light-skinned and very handsome. He also had a girlfriend who had also graduated from U of M, who was working in the Marketing department downtown.

We never crossed the line because of his girlfriend and I was still in love with Brad. Eventually Nick and his girlfriend broke up and things started to change between us.

Darnell Dilworth

Receiving an Achievement Award from two of the District Managers

When the Snowbird Cries

Darnell Dilworth

Chapter 7: A new man in my life

I now have a new relationship in my life, Nick and I are seeing more of each other and he was very good for my ego. He was always complimenting me on how I look, and I loved the way he looked at me. He knew how to dress to impress, he wore three-piece suits every day and the men's cologne he wore was awesome, he smelled so good.

He took me to real fantasy restaurants for dinner, I always felt like a princess when I was out with him. One night he was taking me to dinner and I wanted him to meet my mother. We went by to see her before going out. My mother was really impressed with him, she kept talking about how good he smelled. Nick was the kind of guy that wanted to be the best, wear the best, drive the best.

We talked about Brad a few times, I told him why we broke up, but I did not give him false hope about my feelings. I was still in love with Brad and Nick knew it.

Nick came to my house one day driving a new car, the car was a new brown 280Z. He knew Brad had a Black one. I think Nick was trying to show me that he could have anything that Brad could have. I also knew that he was still in love with the girlfriend he just broke up with. We both were licking our wounds over our failed relationships. Nick and I had gone out for the evening and ended up at his apartment, we got into a conversation as to why I never finished college, why I did not have a college degree. I said it's just the way it is for me, I told him "Life Happened". He sometimes called me by my last name and he said "Ross I am very attracted to you and I love the time we spend together but the only thing that stops me from considering marriage with you is the fact you don't have a college degree. I looked at him and I said, Oh really. I am too stupid for you to marry but I'm not too stupid for you to take to bed.

I got up and asked him to drive me home. He was pleading with me to stay but I was firm, I told him to take my stupid ass home.

When I got to my house I leaped out of his car and went inside my house without saying good-bye. He knew I was furious with him. The next day at work he could see my desk when he stood up. He was so tall he could see over the partition. He tried calling me on my desk phone but when I answered and realized it was him I hung up.

Later that day I returned from lunch and there was a big bouquet of flowers waiting for me on my desk. I opened the card and it was a note from Nick apologizing for what he had said to me. He came over to my desk and asked me to come out in the hall to talk. I went with him, he told me he was wrong to say what he said, and he was very sorry. I told him if that's how you feel and that's what you want you should never settle for anything less. I excepted his apology, but

Darnell Dilworth

we were just friends after that. We never had an intimate relationship ever again, we remained good friends.

He later married the girlfriend from college, although I was invited to his wedding I did not go. Time to time he would come by to visit and vent about something his wife did, I would listen to him and give my advice but that was all he got from me.

One-day Nick called and asked me if I would like to work on a project with him, he said photographers were coming to the office to take pictures for the company paper. I told him I would love to. The project went well, and I had a lot of fun working on it. I was hoping this would get my name out there and I would get noticed by upper management.

I volunteered for a lot of special projects whenever something came my way. I knew I had what it took for a higher position, but I did not have the college background to sell myself. My night school classes helped but my advancement would still be very slow.

When the Snowbird Cries

Nick Harris and me

It was now 1979 and I was still on my own as far as relationships go. I had two girlfriends I grew up with and we spent a lot of time hanging out. I remember we planned a trip to go to Toronto, Canada. It was four of us, Vicki Rice, Denice Cleary, Vicki's friend Geri and myself. We went away for the weekend and we had a great time.

Darnell Dilworth

Whenever I heard about someone having a party I would invite Vicki and Denice to go with me. I remember the three of us going to a party at the Jeffersonian Apartments downtown.

It was a friend of Brad's giving the party. While at the party Brad and I began to talk, and I asked him how was married life. He said it was okay, I left it at that.

A few months later around Christmas time my girlfriend and her son came over for a visit. The boys were in the living room playing and my friend and I were in the dining room talking. Suddenly, my son came running in and said, "Mom that man that drives that black car is on the porch". I went to the door and when I got there he was gone. I looked down and there was a gift-wrapped package laying inside the screen door and storm door.

I opened the card and it was a Christmas gift from Brad, the gift was a pair of Isotoner gloves. Later after my girlfriend left I called him to thank him for the gloves. He asked me if he could come by and see me the next day, I told him it would be okay.

The next day I was excited and nervous at the same time, I had no idea what he wanted. Later after work I left my son at my mother's house and I went home to wait for him. When he came in he grabbed me and kissed me. He held me very close to him and I melted in his arms.

When the Snowbird Cries

He told me how much he missed me and that he and his wife were getting a divorce. He told me it just did not work out. I told him I was still in love with him and I was so glad to see him. We started dating again and again it did not last. Within a year's time he was seeing someone else. I knew then he and I were not meant to be together.

It is now 1978 and I meet a young woman working across the hall her name is Karen Robinson. She was very slim, beautiful and had a wonderful personality. She and I became great friends. She was engaged to be married that year and I was one of her bridesmaids. Sometime later I would sing at her sister's wedding. We have been friends for forty years now.

Chapter 8: Family Gatherings

The holidays were always a time to celebrate at my mother's house, this was a time for the family to come together. When my Dad was alive our house was where the holiday dinner would be held, some of my father's brothers, their wives and children would come over. Although the house was small, we made it work. The dining room was usually where my father and his brothers would eat, my aunts and my mother ate in the living room. The children ate downstairs in the basement.

After my father passed away my mother still had the family over for the holidays. It was a chance for her to gather all her children and grandchildren together under one roof. Muslims did not celebrate Christmas.

By this time none of my mother's children were following the Muslim faith. My mother still regarded herself as Muslim and she followed the teaching up until her passing.

Family dinner at my Mom's house was always a treat, my mother was a fantastic cook. She was from the south and southern cooking was always delicious but not as healthy as it could be. My mother stopped cooking pork after we joined the Mosque. She substituted turkey to flavor things like green beans. She tried to eliminate as much fat as possible.

When the Snowbird Cries

Soul food cooking came about during slavery times, black people did not have a lot to celebrate, so cooking became their way of expressing their love for one another, that's how Sunday dinners came about, it was more than just eating. It was a chance to share your joys and sorrows with each other. A chance to gather, laugh, remember the good old days and those family members who were no longer with us.

Sometimes the gatherings were a lot of fun for me and times they were not. As an adult I still did not like a lot of loud talking and yelling which my family did a lot of. I had two siblings that seem to get into it all the time. They were always challenging each other as to who knew more about a subject than the other. When it became to heated for me I said good-bye to my mother and I went home.

We also went out to dinner as a family to Stanley's in Detroit. It was a Chinese restaurant we all loved. I remember when I was still married a bunch of us went there for dinner. I think it was about twenty of us. It would be more than family; a lot of our friends would go as well.

We would also have barbecues in my Mom's backyard on the fourth of July. My mother began celebrating all her grandchildren's birthdays during that time, she said there were too many of them to remember all their dates.

As my mother's health started to decline I started taking over the holiday dinners, I remember my first family dinner was at my house on Strathmoor in Detroit. I can't remember how well the food turned out, but no one went to the hospital that day.

Family time, was something my mother really cherished. She wanted all her children to remain close. I did not think it would end up being my sole responsibility to carry on the family tradition. My mother had four girls and my sister Mona Lisa moved to Texas but the rest of us stayed in Michigan. Every holiday no one volunteered to have the family dinner. If there was a dinner I would be the one to prepare it.

I was later told by one of my sisters that another sister said she wanted to make her own traditions with her family. I thought we were all family, I even offered to help her if she had the holiday dinner at her house, but it never happened.

It is now 1980 and my career at Michigan Bell Telephone which is now call Ameritech was moving very slowly. By now, I have gone through nine supervisors and five departments. I had more supervisors than departments because once I got comfortable with having a certain supervisor that supervisor would be promoted to another job and then a new person would take their place and I'd start all over again. I am now working in the Outside Plant department located in the Edison Plaza on Bagley in downtown Detroit.

I worked on the fifteenth floor and one day while walking through the

When the Snowbird Cries

lobby a young man followed me and asked me for my name. I told him, and he said his name was Carl. I said hello and went on to my office.

The next day I ran into the same guy and he said good morning and I replied to him. He told me, "we have to stop meeting like this, why don't you let me take you to lunch". I told him, "I don't know you from Adam and I will not go anywhere with you". He said, "I'm harmless, and you can trust me". There was a restaurant in my building called Piper's Alley, so we decided to meet for lunch there.

Later that afternoon I met him at the restaurant and we started to talk. We made small talk about where we grew up and where we went to school. Then the conversation turned to family, I mentioned that most of my family was in Detroit. He said he grew up in California. I started to mention some of my aunts and uncles by name, he looked at me and said I have an uncle by the same name or I have an aunt by that name. I asked him what was his last name, he said it was Walker. I told him my maiden name was Walker, I asked him what is your father's name, he said Arthur Walker, I told him I have an uncle Arthur Walker.

He described his father to me and I said your father's description sounds just like my uncle. When I said I had an aunt Fannie, he said that's my father's sister. I told him she is my father's sister as well.

Darnell Dilworth

We looked at each other and I said, I think you and I are cousins. After lunch I went straight to my office and called my aunt Fannie and I told her what happened, she said you were talking to your uncle Arthur's outside child. That's what they called children born out of wedlock. She decided we all had to meet, so we ended up having a family gathering at my cousin Nadie and Guild's house.

My sisters and my mother were there, I realized then why I was not attracted to him, he was a very handsome guy but there was something that kept me from being interested in him sexually.

I would see Carl from time to time when I came to work and then I did not see him anymore. I later found out he went back to California where he would die of AIDS years later. He died at a very young age, I heard he was infected with AIDS through drug use.

I worked downtown at the Edison Plaza for two years, then I transferred back to the American Motors building in 1981.

I like working in Southfield better than downtown especially because no city taxes were being withheld from my check.

I was living life and one-day a friend of mine invited me to a party. I decided to go and while there she introduced me to a young man by the name of Robert Graham. He was very cute, and he had been watching me all evening.

When the Snowbird Cries

By this time, I am single again and I was not looking for another relationship. He came over to my table and we started talking, we danced, and he finally asked for my phone number. I gave it to him.

I became very fond of Robert who preferred being called Bobby, that's what his family called him. I got to know his family very well and his mother really took a liking to me. She took Arts and Craft classes in the evening. One-night Bobby and I came by for a visit, she handed me a Ceramic Ash Tray that she made in class. She knew I did not smoke but I told her I would use it as a candy dish.

In the fall of 1980 I was asleep, and a dog was barking outside my window. I was still living in the house on Strathmoor in Detroit. The house was a three-bedroom Colonial and all the bedrooms were upstairs with a full bathroom. I did not own a dog, so I just assumed the dog was after a cat or something in the bushes. I looked at the clock and it was about 4:00 a.m., I laid back down and tried to go back to sleep, but I couldn't sleep.

In my mind something was telling me "get up turn on the lights, get up turn on the lights" I finally followed my mind and I got up, went out into the hallway and turned on the lights, at that moment I heard footsteps running from the side of my house. I froze, I did not move for several minutes. I was waiting to see if someone was downstairs.

My son was spending time with his Dad and I was home alone.

I finally started down the stairs checking windows and doors as I moved through the house. I walked through the dining room into the kitchen and opened the door leading to the basement and side door. I turned on the basement light, looked down the stairs and I saw glass all over the floor. Someone had broken out the small window in the basement. It was too small for a grown person to fit through. I slammed the door, locked it and ran to the phone to call the police.

It seemed like it took the police forever to get there but they were at my house in about ten minutes. After calling the police I called Bobby, he lived near seven mile and Ryan in Detroit. He arrived shortly after the police, the police went outside and checked around the back of my house and when they finished they came in and told me who ever it was had been out there for a while trying to get in. They cut through several window screens in the back of the house. There was a small upstairs porch off one of the back bedrooms that had a broken rail. The intruder was trying to climb up to the second floor, but the rail broke.

While at my house the police got a call over their walkie talkie about a B&E (Breaking and Entering) happening down the street from me. They quickly left and told me they would be back. An hour later the police were back, they asked me if I saw anyone. I told them no, the person ran away as soon as I turned on the lights. They told me a man had broken in a home down the street with a woman and several kids inside.

When the Snowbird Cries

He did not hurt anyone he just asked for money and left. The police took a report and left. I was so scared; Bobby and I slept with the lights on. The next day I called Guardian Alarm and had bars put on all the windows. I sold the house the following year and moved to an Apartment in Oak Park, Michigan. I believed a guardian angel was watching over me that night, I think it was my Dad.

I dated Bobby for about a year when someone else caught my eye. Shortly after moving to Oak Park Bobby and I were over.

Me, Bobby, Henriette (who passed away 2010), and her husband)

Chapter 9: The Eighties

My son and I are now settled in our new home at the Northgate apartments. My son is enrolled in Berkley High and has adjusted well to the all-white school. His grades are excellent, he is bringing home A's and B's. He quickly makes a new friend who lives in the same complex and I was happy he was adjusting to his new surroundings.

Soon after moving in my new apartment Ameritech goes on strike and I am assigned strike duty in Pontiac, Michigan. The picketers were ruthless. I worked twelve hours a day, six days a week. One day I was done with my shift and it was time to leave. The supervisor told everyone to get ready and we could follow her out of the parking lot. The picketers were not allowed on the parking lot only outside the gate.

I was hurrying trying to get ready, so I would not end up being the last car out, I was not fast enough. I ended up being the last car and the picketers surrounded me. They rocked my car, beat on the windows and hood. They called me names and I was so scared. I finally got out of the driveway and started down the street. When I got home I called our boss's District Secretary and told her I was not going back. She told me to take the next day off and I would get a call later letting me know where to report.

When the Snowbird Cries

I ended up at my regular office and the experience was much better.

Sometime later I started dating the Engineer I met when I first hired into the company in 1971. His name was Raymond Dilworth. He had divorced his wife two years earlier.

His strike assignment was just down the street from where I lived. We would meet at my apartment for lunch and shoot the breeze until time to go back to work. When I started the company I was engaged, when I was getting a divorced he was getting married. We were two ships always passing in the night.

We started dating on a regular basis and before I knew it I was hooked on him. Raymond had a lot of the qualities I was looking for in a man. He was kind, gentle and down to earth, also very handsome. He had a five-year-old son and my son was eleven.

We were spending a lot of time with each other and when he got his son for visitation, we would do things together. I remember it was my son's birthday and he was crazy about Michael Jackson. I decided to take him to the Jackson five Victory Tour concert at the Silverdome in Pontiac, Michigan. Raymond and I thought it would be cute to take the boys dressed in their Michael Jackson jackets.

I took off work one day to stand in line for the tickets. I was in line by 7:00 a.m. in the morning. I never thought it would be an all-day process. It was July and it was very hot, and I did not get to the ticket booth until around 2:00 p.m. in the afternoon. I was so hot and tired when I got home but it was worth it to see my son's face when I told him we were going to the concert.

We took the boys to the concert and they had a good time. Of course, they had to have the Souvenir books (which I still have today), the white glove, etc.

We would spend as much time as we could together with our boys when we both had our shared visitations.

My relationship with Raymond was moving along fine. He took me to meet his mother in Ohio one weekend and I was excited and nervous at the same time.

I liked her from the start, she was very easy to talk to and I think she really liked me. After many visits, we started talking to each other on the phone. She had a lot of values that were like my own.

I had fallen in love with Raymond, there was something about him that made me feel safe. I was at ease around him, he was easy to talk to and there was no pretend with him. I said to myself, could this man be the one God made for me, I started thinking about marriage again. I felt I had found the right person this time. I decided to bring up the subject about marriage to see how he felt about it. In a casual way I asked him if he ever thought about getting married again, he told me that would never happen again.

When the Snowbird Cries

I was surprised he felt that way. I did not want to waste my time with someone who did not want to get married. I told him I would like to get married again someday. THAT WAS A BIG MISTAKE.

Our relationship took a different turn after that. I started seeing less of him. Then I found out he was seeing another woman. I knew of a woman he met in Chicago after separating from his ex-wife that was still in his life.

I was the kind of woman who wanted monogamous relationships. I could not let myself be part of a tri-angle, we broke up.

During this time, I made the decision to have a tubal ligation. I used my older sister's doctor to have it done because my GYN was from the old school of thought, he said I was too young and one day I will want to have more children. I did it anyway. I felt Mr. Right was not coming.

It's 1987 and I am now working at the Onyx Plaza in Southfield. I purchased a home in Oak Park, I was tired of living in an apartment and Oak Park was near the area where I grew up.

I wanted my son to stay at Berkley High School because he was doing so well there. My neighbor in the complex let me use her address as his home of residence. That worked out until my son did something in school that caused a note to be sent home. The mailman knew my neighbor and he sent the envelope back to the school.

Darnell Dilworth

I received a call at work and after speaking with his counselor I was told if I wanted him to remain at Berkley High I would have to pay a non-residence tuition fee. I could not afford it, so I had to pull him out of Berkley and he started attending Oak Park High school.

My son's grades started to fall he was no longer getting A's and B'. I noticed his mood was changing as well, I had no idea what was going on with him.

One day he came to me and asked me "Mom is there something wrong with Dad" I asked him, "what do you mean" he told me he found magazines of naked men in his father's dresser.

I told my ex-husband when we divorced I would never do anything to interfere with his relationship with his son. I would never tell him why we divorced or anything about his father's lifestyle. I told my ex-husband when my son was old enough he would have to tell him the truth about himself and why we divorced. I called his Dad on the phone and said, "the day to tell your son about yourself is today". I thought his Dad would come over and talk to his son face to face. Instead, he talked to both of us over the speakerphone.

After the phone call with his Dad I tried to reassure my son that his father's lifestyle had nothing to do with how his father loved him. My son seemed to except what I said that day. After the divorce from my ex-husband I had been carrying around guilt about marrying a homosexual man and bringing a child into that situation. Why did I not see it before I got married? The answer was I was too young and inexperienced.

I wanted so badly to marry again and have more children. I wanted to give my son the family he deserved, with a father and mother under the same roof. But life saw things differently.

I was still struggling to climb that corporate ladder. I've had several supervisors by this time who were acting as my sponsor. I saw a lot of females with my same level of education being promoted to management, but I was not willing to sleep my way to the top.

Darnell attending a meeting in Chicago, IL in 1988

Darnell Dilworth

Once a year the company gave a big banquet they called it "Boss's Night". It was a night when managers would take their secretaries and clerks to dinner. I was reporting to Leo Ogden at that time. He was an older gentleman who was very nice and respectful. I enjoyed that evening very much.

It had been rumored that Boss's Night was a night deals were made. There were some women who had no problem sleeping with a manager to get ahead in the company. I was not one of them.

There were days when I got home I just wanted to sit down, watch news on TV and chill for a moment. My son wanted to play but I was not in the mood. Sometimes I would play with him and other times I would have him go to his bedroom and watch TV. At times I felt so guilty.

I had a girlfriend whose son was two weeks younger than my son, they were like brothers. I would let him come over and spend the night, they would have a good time playing together.

I started to realize being an only child was very lonely for him. I grew up in a household with five other siblings. I felt my decision to have my tubes tied may have been a mistake.

I would make a special effort to do things with my son. We went roller skating, the movies, theme parks, and the zoo. I buried myself in work and family.

When the Snowbird Cries

1978 - Boss's Night
My Manager - Outside Plant Group
Leo Ogden and Darnell Ross

One of my favorite Supervisors

Chapter 10: Growing Pains

The eighties were coming to an end and my siblings and I decide to give my mother a combination birthday and retirement surprise party April 1989 at the Westin hotel in Southfield. We rented a ballroom for about fifty people and my younger sister and her husband put a band together for us to put on a show for my Mom. It was a wonderful night and my mother had a great time.

A new decade had just begun, and I am eager to see what's in store for me and my son. He is now a teenage who is starting to defy me. He had been asking me for a dog and I finally gave in. I found a three-year-old Sheltie in Allen Park from the newspaper. The man who was selling the dog was from Florida and he had moved into a condo in Sterling Heights that did not allow pets. A relative in Allen Park was keeping the dog for him until he could sell him.

I did not know much about Allen Park but a co-worker I worked with did. She and I went to see the dog one day after work and when I saw him I fell in love right away. He was a bit shy at first but quickly warmed up to me. The dog was house broken and could perform a few commands. I ended up buying the dog to surprise my son. We decided to name him Dusty.

When the Snowbird Cries

My son and Dusty became buddies and I gave him the responsibility for Dusty's care. After three weeks my son was slacking off on caring for the dog. I would come home from work and the dog had not been fed, he needed to go out to relieve himself and being a long-haired dog, he needed to be brushed every day.

It soon became clear that I was going to be the one to care for the dog and I did not need that responsibility on top of everything else. I kept Dusty for a year and then I sold him to a grandfather from Flat Rock who was buying the dog for his granddaughter.

Darnell Dilworth

My son celebrated his sweet sixteenth birthday in 1988 and I now have a teenager in the house.

During this time Rap music is popular and my son was listening to that music. I hated it and I still do. We battled over what kind of Rap music would be played in my house. I thought my son's rebellion may have been caused by his feelings about his father. I would try talking to him about his feeling, but he would just shut me down. I discovered he was skipping school and hiding his report cards. I went to PTA meetings and spoke to his teachers. One of his teachers told me, he could get A' and B's in her class but he only does just enough to not fail. I spoke to him about his grades and he told me only Nerds get good grades, I knew then it was peer pressure that was guiding my son's personality (The dummy down theory). I did not want to pick his friends, but it was clear to me he was associating with the wrong kids in school. He was becoming defiant and not listening to me. I felt it was time for me to try tough love. I put him out and he went to his Dad's house.

When he began living with his Dad his grades improved. He was getting A's and B' again. I discovered my ex-husband was using corporal punishment.

It's 1990, my son celebrates his eighteenth birthday and he graduates from Oak Park High. To my surprise he signs up for the Marines. My heart was broken, my ex-husband and I wanted our son to attend college after graduating from high school. Although my ex-husband and I were not meant to be, he was an excellent father. He had been saving for my son's college education since my son was three years old. When my son graduated from high school his father had money in the bank to pay for all four years of my son's college education, but he decided to go to the Marines.

Darnell Dilworth

It was peace time and I did not feel my son would be in any danger and that made me feel better about his decision.

When the Snowbird Cries

Time goes on and one day I came home and got the mail from my mail box. I looked through the mail and I saw a letter from my son. In the first paragraph he told me if you are standing sit down. My son told me I was about to become a grandmother. The baby was due very soon. I was shocked. At forty years old I was going to be a grandmother. The baby was born, and my son was the proud father of a baby girl. They name her Brittany Marie Ross. I did not know the mother of my granddaughter. I later found out she lived around the corner from me in Oak Park.

My son finished his basic training and was honorable dismiss due to physical problems with his legs. My son came home and then decided he wanted to attend college. My ex-husband and I were so happy, and his Dad still had the money he had saved for my son's education. My son was enrolled in Western Michigan University in Kalamazoo, Michigan and was staying in Davison hall. He was now settled, and I was expecting him to really do well. My son quit after one semester.

Devastated does not begin to describe how I was feeling, but it was his life to live as he chose. I saw my granddaughter on occasion, but my son was no longer involved with the mother and I didn't really know her at all.

Years later my son met and married another young woman I had never met. They moved to Indiana and had a son they would name

Michael. The marriage was over in two years. My son chose his own path and I will have to respect it.

As time moves on, after a long day at work I come home and retrieve the mail from the mailbox I saw something that looked like a greeting card. It was from Raymond, it was a "I miss you card" I was so happy to hear from him again. I called him to thank him for the card and we talked for a long time on the phone. We decided to make a date to go out for dinner the next day. Raymond told me he missed me and did not want to let me go. We both had strong feelings for each other. We started dating again and we fell in love all over again. In 1993 we decided to take a trip to Hawaii, by this time I had been to Hawaii twice already, once with my ex-husband in 1974 an again in 1986 with Raymond's mother. I thought what a great place to rekindle our relationship. We had a great time in Hawaii, I only wish it was my honeymoon with him. He had not changed his mind about marriage and neither did I. We dated for a year and then we broke again.

When the Snowbird Cries

I started working downtown again in the Headquarters building on Cass Ave. and Michigan Ave. The people I worked with were always involved in office gossip or arguments. I was so unhappy working in that department. I stayed to myself and I was truly alone. I had a few friends who worked in other departments and we would get together for coffee and go out for lunch.

I started working on the weekends even though I was not being paid. It gave me a chance to stay busy and prevent backlog.

One day my supervisor called me to her desk and asked me if I had been in the office that past Sunday. I told her yes, I was told that one of the women looked at the last login list on their MAC computer and she saw my last login was on a Sunday.

I told my supervisor I was just getting caught up on some work and I did not expect to get paid for it. I had time on my hands and I decided to come into the office.

My supervisor praised me for my diligence but because I was a non-management employee, she could not let me work without be paying me.

I had a computer at home and I asked her would it be a problem if I took work home. She said no but I would need a SecurID card to be able to connect to the company systems from home. I filled out the paperwork to apply for the SecurID card, a few weeks later it was mailed to my supervisor. Now I could work from home and I had no problems until one of the workers in my office found out I had a card. The office trouble makers caused so much trouble that my General Manager ended up coming from Southfield to the office downtown to settle the situation. In the meeting it was made clear to the union that what I was doing was voluntary and anyone who wanted to work from home could apply for a SecurID card, then the issue was not everyone can afford a home computer. My GM settled that issue by making a suitcase type computer (large laptop for the 1990's) available for checkout to who ever wanted it.

As you can imagine, no one applied for a card and no one checked out the computer. What the people in my office did not realize was they were my best source of advertisement. I wanted to get noticed by upper management and now I was. My name was on the lips of my supervisor, my District level and my General Manager and in a good way. I was now known for my enthusiasm, work ethic and being self-motivated.

I ended up being transferred to the complex where I started twenty-four years earlier, the Northwest Office Complex in Southfield. I was the District Manager's Assistant. It was still a non-management position, but it paid a little more money. I had a cubical all to myself because I handled very sensitive information.

When the Snowbird Cries

Chapter 11: A Great Lady is Gone

It is now 1996 and my mother's health is starting to decline. Her eyesight is failing, and we finally had to insist she give up her car keys. I eventually became my mother's Guardian and Fiduciary, the person who would take care of her medical needs, money and other assets.

My younger brother was living there at the time, but he was working during the day and that left my Mom home alone. The office I worked out of was nearby, so I could sometimes drop by and check on her. I always called her on my lunch hours. I arranged for a lift chair to helped her with standing from a seated position. My Mom soon lost the use of her legs and could no longer walk. I believe my mother suffer a minor stroke and she was now bed ridden. The plan was to keep my mother in her home, but it was becoming more difficult by the day. I would sit at my desk at work and ask God what should I do, how should I handle this. I approached my mother with an idea to move her in with me. I told her I would sell the house, move her in with me and use the proceeds to hire a daycare nurse to take care of her while I was working. My mother did not like that idea, she wanted to leave the house to all her children. When my grandmother passed away my mother found out she was cheated out of her inheritance by a friend of my grandmother. She was tricked into making the friend her beneficiary and Power of Attorney over my grandmother's affairs. My grandmother owned a grocery store and an apartment building at the time. My mother and father could not afford a long court battle.

I eventually dropped the idea and my mother remain in her home. I was working with a social worker who informed me that I could get a hospital bed delivered to the house by getting a prescription from her doctor.

One day I called my mother to see how she was doing, the phone rang and then I her a big thump. I called for my Mom to answer but I did not hear anything. I went to my boss and told her I had to leave my Mom was in trouble.

When I got to her house and let myself in, I went to her bedroom and I found her on the floor, the phone was underneath her. The bed rail had been left down, and she had rolled out of the bed. I called out to her, but she did not answer me. I immediately call 911 and an ambulance was there quickly.

She was taken to the hospital and spent three weeks there. The social worker I was working with told me she could not go back to her house unless we had a daycare nurse to care for her.

I spoke to my oldest sister and we both decided that the best thing for her would be a nursing home. We started searching together, I found a place called Botsford Common in Farmington Hills. I went there and was given a tour. The facility was great, I loved it. There was independent living as well as assisted living. There were onsite nurses and doctors on call. They had an onsite beauty salon, café, etc. The one problem was my mother was not a resident of Farmington Hills and the cost was well over what we could afford. My sister and I found a place in Southfield and they excepted her social security check as well as the state's contribution. I believe when we took the tour of the facility they only showed us the best parts. We decided to place my Mom at that facility. The social worker advised me to make sure there were no restricted hours and we could visit whenever we wanted. That way we could observe how they were taking care of my Mom.

My mother had been there about a week. I stopped by after work one day and when I got to her room she was not there. I went to the nurse's station and asked, "where was my Mom" I was told she was taken to the dining room to socialize with the other residents. By this time my mother could not sit up in a chair by herself, I went to the dining room and there she was slump over in a wheelchair, a few buttons on her pajama shirt were open and part of her breast was exposed.

I immediately took her back to her room and picked her up and placed her in the lift chair we bought from home. Her dinner tray was there, so I prepared to feed her. I looked at the food and it was not what was on her food card and it was cold. I went down to the nurse's station to complain, I said "my mother's card says she should have meat as part of her meal, there is no meat". The lady told me "meat is a protein and so is macaroni". I said this food is cold and I am not going to feed my mother cold food. She said, "there is a microwave in the dining room".

I went to the dining room and found the microwave, opened the door and it was filthy. I threw the tray on the table and went back to my mother's room, by this time my younger brother Glenn was there. I told him to watch Mom while I go get her something decent to eat.

I went to a restaurant not far away and purchased a dinner. I came back and fed her. That was it for me, I called my older sister Carol and told her we had to get my mother out that place.

We discussed it and decided to talk to my younger sister and her husband to find out if my mother could move in with them. She had a daughter who had just graduated from high school and was not working. I thought it would be perfect for my mother to be with family.

The social worker told me by having a family member as her caregiver the state would pay the caregiver instead of a nursing home. My sister and her husband agreed. We took my mother out of the facility and transported her to my sister's home.

My sister and her family took excellent care of my mom. I always loved and respected them for the sacrifice their family made. My mother seems to thrive at my sister's but eventually her health became worst and she had to be admitted to the hospital. My Mom soon fell into a comma.

My mother finally succumbed to her illness and passed away March 1998. The same day my Mom passed away my District Manager told me I had been promoted to Project Manager. I finally reached the goal I worked so hard to achieve. My manager told me to take care of what I needed to and if she could be of any help let her know.

My mother use to tell me she always dreamed of coming to where I work and seeing my name on an office door. I came close, my name was on an office partitioned cubical.

Twelve days before my mother passed away to my surprise Raymond finally proposed to me at a Primerica convention at the Hyatt Regency on March 5, 1998, in front of our Primerica team and my sister Carol. I was so happy I could hardly speak. I never had the chance to tell my Mother that her daughter was in love again and was getting married.

I needed to mourn but there was no time, arrangements had to be made for my mother's funeral. We had my mother's service at Cole's funeral home in Detroit and she was laid to rest at Woodlawn Cemetery on Woodward in Detroit.

Life seems to stand still when someone you love has left you. They say life goes on, but it hurts just the same.

When the Snowbird Cries

My Mom

Chapter 12: A New Marriage and Farwell

It is June 1998 and I'm busy planning my wedding. I am still mourning the loss of my mother, but I know she is still with me. I am now working as a Project Manager and I am very busy with my job and trying to sell my house in Oak Park. Raymond and I decided to build a house of our own and we located a site in Southfield. Raymond's cousin was our realtor so that made everything so much easier.

We decide on a modest wedding with mostly family and a few friends. We were married July 1998 at a church in Southfield, I was the happiest woman alive. I loved Raymond so much and I knew he loved me. I finally had the man I was supposed to be with, my life partner.

Our honeymoon was postponed because we were trying to get the house built. My house in Oak Park was put up for sale on a Monday and by that Saturday it was sold. I had no idea it would sell so fast. I had ninety days to move out. We had a garage sale which went very well.

Raymond moved back into his childhood home located in Detroit after his father passed away in 1995. I moved in with him after the wedding to wait for the completion of our home. We were hoping the house would be ready the year of our wedding but that did not materialize.

When the Snowbird Cries

The house was completed in 1999 and we closed July 1999. I now had a new marriage, new home and a new job. All was right with the world.

A year after Raymond and I got married he decided that his mother could no longer live on her own out in California. She had been diagnosed with macular degeneration, which is an eye disease. She could still live on her own but needed special eyeglasses to see.

We purchased a condo around the corner from our home, that way she would be close by and we could keep an eye on her. I took her to her doctor's appointments, ran errands, and on the weekends, I would come over clean her house and do her laundry. It was working out well until Raymond and I became real busy at work.

Raymond was a second level manager in the IT department. He was responsible for the Data Center Operations and Support, with 50 first level managers reporting to him. He was responsibility for fourteen data centers spread over six states.

I on the other hand started out my management career as a Project manager working with other managers on major projects. After my first year I was given the assignment of Plug-in Supervisor managing seven Technical Specialist who worked outside the office performing central office inventories and four general clerks who were in the office with me. I handled that assignment well until a manager in Ohio

Darnell Dilworth

was fired and I was asked to take over his subordinates until a new manager was found. My responsibilities increased by five. I now had the responsibility of sixteen employees who were located across six cities and two states.

Raymond was working long hours, he was on call 24/7, I was out of town a lot visiting my subordinates in the other locations.

Raymond and I both traveled for our jobs, we both built up a lot of SkyMiles with Delta. The company started to cut back on-air travel and I was assigned a company car, so I spent a lot of time on the road between states driving. Raymond however was still flying from time to time.

One day in September 2001 I was sitting at my desk and one of the clerks out on the floor had a radio on, suddenly, I her loud voices and people gasping. I came out of my cubicle and went over to listen to the radio. A plane had just hit the World Trade center in New York. Everyone was in shock, I ran back to my cubicle and pull up MSNBC on my computer. There it was, the building was on fire. As I sat at my computer watching everything unfold, another plane hit the other tower. I could not believe my eyes, I called Raymond to see if he had heard about, but he was not in his office. I was calm because I knew he was out of the office taking care of personal business. As I continued to watch the news on my computer, another plane hit the Pentagon and that's when a lot of the people in my office lost it.

When the Snowbird Cries

Some were saying they needed to go home to be with their families. They were all acting like the world was coming to an end. I guess in some ways it was. I will never forget that day.

After five years of marriage Raymond's mother was becoming more demanding, she was feeling neglected. It started to cause a rift between she and I and my relationship with my husband. We were like to ships passing in the night. When I was home I was running back and forth between two houses. My sex life with my husband was none existent.

Darnell Dilworth

My mother-in-law became ill and needed surgery. She came through the surgery without any complications but could not go back to her home. When she left the hospital, she came home with us. She was not confined to her bed, but she still needed someone to help with her personal needs. I usually got home before Raymond, so a lot of her care fell on me.

Raymond and I had no privacy or time to ourselves and I felt something would have to give or our marriage was not going to survive. I think Raymond felt it too, because he came to me and told me he spoke to his sister who lived in Phoenix, Arizona about taking their mother in to live with her and her husband. She agreed and within a month's time she was gone.

Raymond and I had a long talk after his mother left for Arizona and we both wanted our marriage to survive. I loved him, and he loved me. We started making special time for our relationship outside of work. That's when Date Night was introduced. Every Friday or Saturday we would make plans to go out. We sometime just went out for dinner and a movie or we would check into a hotel for the weekend. We were boaters and had a 38 ft. Carver Santego, so we would go on boating trips with other boaters in our marina. We began to take two trips a year out of town with our close friends. We went to places like Cancun, Hawaii, Porta Rico, Aruba, Florida, Las Vegas, St Martin, etc. Life was good between Raymond and I and our jobs were leveling off.

When the Snowbird Cries

In 2006 Raymond and I made the decision to retire from the company after thirty-six years for Raymond and thirty-five years for me. Rumors were starting to spread about changes to the pension plan and medical, we wanted to leave before any of that took place. Raymond retired in April and I retired in June.

As time moved on Raymond's mother's health starts to fail. She was diagnosed with heart failure. She was a smoker and she smoked up until she passed away February 2010.

My husband and his sister who lived in Phoenix had a memorial service for their mother in Michigan. I stood by my husband through his grief as he did when my mother passed away. Our marriage was and still is solid as a rock.

Raymond and his Mom

Darnell Dilworth

Early in January of 2012, I had been missing my sister who lived in Texas. I decided to call her to find out if she would like to come for a visit. She loved the idea but could not afford to make the trip. I told her not to worry about the cost, I would talk to my other siblings and find out if they would be willing to chip in and buy her a ticket. I spoke to my older sister Carol, brothers Adolph and Glenn and we all decided to buy her a plane ticket to come home. She wanted to wait until her granddaughter was out of school and then she could come. We planned the trip for June 2012.

On May 12, 2012, it was a beautiful day outside. Raymond and I decide to take the boat out for a cruise on the river. My brother Adolph was retired so I call him up and ask him if he would like to join us. He told me he would love to go. Raymond went to the store to buy snacks for our day on the river, I went to pick up my brother and bring him back to my house. My brother and I are sitting in my Livingroom when Raymond came back from the store and we all were just sitting around talking when the phone rang. It was my niece Kimberly who lived in Texas, she said "Auntie Aunt Mona is dead, she died in her sleep". My sister was gone, I could not believe it. She died in her sleep at age 59. She had been ill for many years with different things, but I had just spoke to her two days before. She told me she had been diagnosed with a disease called sarcoidosis, but she said she felt fine and still wanted to make the trip to Michigan.

When the Snowbird Cries

After recovering from the shock, I was on a plane to Texas within an hour. My niece Kimberly was there to meet me at the airport and we went straight to my sister's place.

My plan was to retrieve my sister's body and fly her back to Michigan for burial. I discovered my sister never divorced her second husband Dwayne and he had final say so over any arrangements, he wanted her funeral and burial in Texas.

The funeral home Dwayne was dealing with was only worried about how much insurance money my sister had and he was trying to spend every penny. My sister left behind two adult children and grandchildren. I was sure she wanted to leave them something.

I was devastated that I had no say in the arrangements. My niece Kimberly came to me and said Dwayne's brother offered another option. He spoke to Dwayne and convinced him to have a funeral service in Texas which would allow all her friends and family to say good-bye and then let me take her body home to rest in peace next to our mother. Dwayne agreed, so we had the service at Golden Gate funeral. They supplied the casket, obituaries, flowers and made the arrangements with Delta Airlines for me to fly back on the same plane with my sister's body.

Meanwhile, my husband is in Michigan making the funeral arrangements for another funeral service and my sister's burial site at Woodlawn. We had the service and my sister was laid to rest next to

Darnell Dilworth

my mother. Later when I was alone I let it go, I cried. I prayed to God to watch over the rest of my family. I never thought just two years later I would have to do it all over again.

It's May 2014, Raymond and I have purchased a new boat. The boat was up north, and we were preparing to bring it down to the Detroit River. We were going up north every weekend getting things ready.

It was a Sunday afternoon and we were on our way back from up north when we received a call from my younger brother Glenn.

He told us my sister Carol was in the hospital. I told him we were on the road and would not be there for another two hours. When we finally arrived at the hospital my sister was conscious and talking to everyone. Later that evening she had to be air lifted to the University Hospital of Michigan in Ann Arbor. My sister had suffered an Aortic Dissection and needed surgery. My brother Adolph and I drove there and got there after she arrived. We spent the night in the waiting room hoping to hear good news once she was out of surgery. Around 7:00 a.m. the doctor came out and said my sister suffered a stroke while in surgery and would never recovery. She suffered brain damage. My brother and I cried together, our hearts were broken.

It was a lot to deal with, but life was not going to let us go just yet. My uncle Arthur who was my father's youngest brother and last sibling passed away June 2014.

When the Snowbird Cries

My sister Carol died July 2014. She was there when my husband proposed to me, she was there for every holiday dinner, she was there when Raymond and I renew our wedding vows, she was there whenever I asked her to be.

My sister Carol had grown children that would make the decisions regarding her funeral. One day I got a call from my niece, she asked me to help handle the services and burial. I told her I would be there for them.

My Mom, my sisters Mona and Carol are buried next to each other. I think that's what they would have wanted.

Throughout my life I have lived to see many changes in the world. Race relations is still a factor these days, but not in my family. I have biracial nephews, nieces, cousins and my own grandson. My husband's family is of mixed race. We are truly a melting pot.

I know God has been with me throughout my life. Every decision, mistake, achievement and hardship, God has been there watching over me. Life is a journey and I am blessed to know I will walk through this journey with my husband Raymond, family and friends.

Truly, life is a journey, of joy and sorrow. No guarantee for happiness, in every tomorrow. Always be prepared for, both defeat and victory, and rely on God's promise to keep you company

When the Snowbird Cries

Every night in my dreams I see you, I feel you

That's how I know you, go on.

Near, far, wherever you are

I believe in my heart the love does, go on and on

~Celine Dion~

Darnell Dilworth

My grandchildren

Granddaughter Brittany

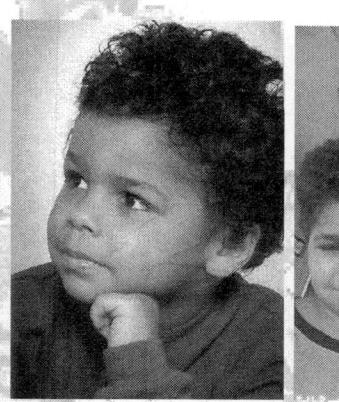

Grandson Michael & his Dad (My Son)

Our granddaughter Rayanna

Our New Granddaughter Riley

The Walker family (Me seated bottom left)

Darnell Dilworth

My husband Raymond and me, we renewed our vows June 2011.
We will celebrate 20 years of marriage July 2018

When the Snowbird Cries